Ben Runs

words by Josephine Croser
illustrated by Sue O'Loughlin

Ben runs.

He runs with a car.

He runs with a bike.

He runs with a boat.

He runs with a train.

He runs with a jet.

He runs with a dog.

He runs with a cat.

He runs with a ball.

He runs with a paddle.

He runs with a hat.

"Ben," says Mom.

"Fix this mess."

"I can not," says Ben.

"I am sleepy."